BEHIND THE BRAND
STAR WARS

BY PAIGE V. POLINSKY

BELLWETHER MEDIA • MINNEAPOLIS, MN

This is not an official Star Wars book. It is not approved by or connected with Star Wars.

This edition first published in 2023 by Bellwether Media, Inc.

No part of this publication may be reproduced in whole or in part without written permission of the publisher.
For information regarding permission, write to Bellwether Media, Inc., Attention: Permissions Department,
6012 Blue Circle Drive, Minnetonka, MN 55343.

Library of Congress Cataloging-in-Publication Data

LC record for Star Wars available at: https://lccn.loc.gov/2022049472

Text copyright © 2023 by Bellwether Media, Inc. BLASTOFF! DISCOVERY and associated logos are trademarks and/or registered trademarks of Bellwether Media, Inc.

Editor: Betsy Rathburn   Designer: Andrea Schneider

Printed in the United States of America, North Mankato, MN.

TABLE OF CONTENTS

A NEW MOVIE	4
A LONG TIME AGO...	6
THE STORY CONTINUES	18
USING THE FORCE	24
CELEBRATING STAR WARS	26
GLOSSARY	30
TO LEARN MORE	31
INDEX	32

A NEW MOVIE

STAR WARS DAY

Star Wars Day is an unofficial holiday held each year on May 4. It was first held in Toronto, Canada, in 2011. Today, fans around the world celebrate!

A family is excited to see the newest Star Wars movie. Before they go to the movie theater, they rewatch past movies to remember what happened. Then, they get ready to go. They each wear their favorite Star Wars shirts and hats. One family member even carries a toy lightsaber.

At the theater, other fans have dressed up, too. The family buys snacks and settles into their seats. Soon, the lights go dark. Star Wars music begins to play. Then, the action begins. Star Wars movies delight audiences around the world!

LIGHTSABER

A LONG TIME AGO...

STAR WARS TOYS

LUCASFILM HEADQUARTERS

Star Wars is one of the most successful entertainment **brands** of all time. It began as a **space opera** movie series created by writer and **director** George Lucas. Today, the company Lucasfilm makes new movies for the **franchise**. Lucasfilm **headquarters** is in San Francisco, California. The brand is owned by the Walt Disney Company.

Star Wars features more than 10 movies, 20 TV series, and hundreds of books! In addition, the brand has earned billions of dollars from selling toys, puzzles, video games, and more!

DARTH JUNIOR

Scientists have named many organisms after the Star Wars franchise. *Darthvaderum greensladeae* is a scary-looking mite named after Darth Vader!

LUCASFILM HEADQUARTERS

SAN FRANCISCO, CALIFORNIA

George Lucas started Lucasfilm in 1971. He and former classmate Gary Kurtz wanted to make a thrilling action movie. They tried to bring the superhero Flash Gordon to the big screen. But the character's **rights** were too expensive.

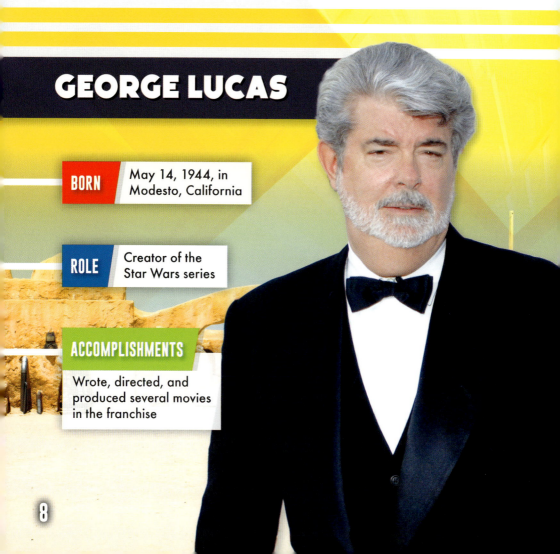

GEORGE LUCAS

BORN
May 14, 1944, in Modesto, California

ROLE
Creator of the Star Wars series

ACCOMPLISHMENTS
Wrote, directed, and produced several movies in the franchise

In April 1973, George began writing his own story. It followed the adventures of characters in a faraway **galaxy**. At the time, similar movies were often dark and grim. But George and Gary were inspired by westerns and fairytales from their childhood. They developed the story into an exciting space fantasy. In time, it was named *Star Wars*.

BEHIND THE SCENES OF *STAR WARS*

At first, George and Gary could not find support for the movie. Movie companies thought it would fail. Finally, Twentieth Century Fox agreed to take a chance. George made a deal that gave him control of *Star Wars* and its **sequels**. He would also control the movie's products.

10

George finished writing *Star Wars* in March of 1975. A few months later, he founded Industrial Light & Magic. This company handled the movie's **special effects**. It made spaceships, creatures, and faraway planets look real. It used new camera technology to bring *Star Wars* to life!

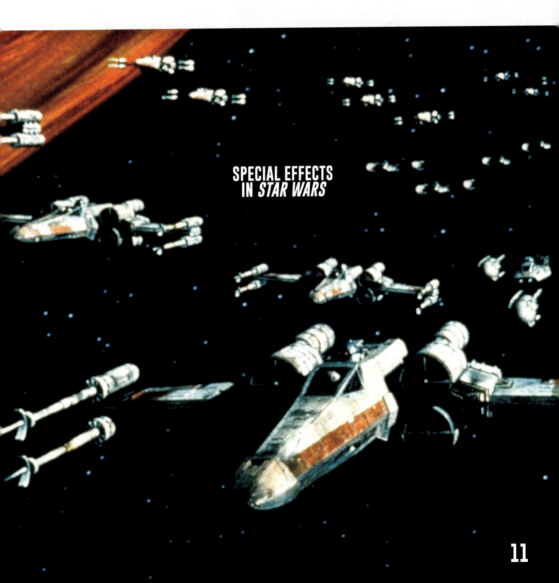

SPECIAL EFFECTS IN *STAR WARS*

Star Wars was released on May 25, 1977. It followed the story of Luke Skywalker as he joined the Rebel **Alliance** in its fight against the Galactic **Empire**. Audiences rooted for Luke as he learned the ways of the Force from his teacher, Obi-Wan Kenobi. They cheered on favorite characters such as the daring pilots Han Solo and Chewbacca, the helpful droid R2-D2, and the brave leader Princess Leia Organa.

STAR WARS DROIDS

R2-D2
First Appeared: *A New Hope*

C-3PO
First Appeared: *A New Hope*

BB-8
First Appeared: *The Force Awakens*

K-2SO
First Appeared: *Rogue One*

D-O
First Appeared: *The Rise of Skywalker*

QUEEN BEHIND THE SCENES

Film editor Marcia Lucas edited the first three Star Wars films. She is responsible for many favorite moments. In 1978, she won an Academy Award for her editing work!

Star Wars earned a record-breaking $307 million in ticket sales. In 1978, it was nominated for ten Academy Awards. It won six. The movie's exciting story and fast-paced action won many fans!

STAR WARS: EPISODE V – THE EMPIRE STRIKES BACK

JEDI MASTER YODA

George used his *Star Wars* earnings to pay for the next two movies himself. *Star Wars: Episode V – The Empire Strikes Back* was released on May 21, 1980. Fans lined up to watch Luke learn about the ways of the Force from Jedi Master Yoda. It was that year's top-earning movie!

Episode VI – Return of the Jedi was released on May 25, 1983. The final movie in the **trilogy** introduced Jabba the Hutt and the Ewoks of planet Endor. It earned a record-breaking $6.2 million on opening day and more than $252 million total!

A NEW NAME

After the success of *Star Wars*, it became clear that more movies would follow. The first movie was renamed to *Star Wars: Episode IV – A New Hope*.

JABBA THE HUTT IN *STAR WARS: EPISODE VI – RETURN OF THE JEDI*

EWOKS

The Star Wars trilogy launched a world of products. Kenner Products sold millions of action figures. Fans loved playing with mini versions of their favorite characters. Toy lightsabers, trading cards, and board games were also popular.

EARLY STAR WARS EARNINGS

Film	Year	Box Office Sales
A NEW HOPE	1977	$307,263,857
THE EMPIRE STRIKES BACK	1980	$209,398,025
RETURN OF THE JEDI	1983	$252,583,617
THE PHANTOM MENACE	1999	$431,088,295
ATTACK OF THE CLONES	2002	$302,191,252
REVENGE OF THE SITH	2005	$380,270,577

Toy sales were strong in the early 1980s. The spin-off TV shows *Ewoks* and *Droids* kept fans entertained. Books and comic series did, too. But without new films, toy sales slowly dropped. In 1985, Kenner stopped making new Star Wars toys. The brand was becoming less popular.

THE STORY CONTINUES

ANAKIN SKYWALKER IN *EPISODE I – THE PHANTOM MENACE*

JAR JAR BINKS

Fans soon had more Star Wars to look forward to. In 1994, George announced a Star Wars **prequel** trilogy. The first movie, *Episode I – The Phantom Menace*, was released in 1999. Viewers followed Anakin Skywalker's early life on the planet Tatooine. Filmmakers used **CGI** technology to bring the movie to life. Jar Jar Binks was among the first fully CGI characters in any movie!

18

The next movie, *Episode II – Attack of the Clones*, was released in 2002. *Episode III – Revenge of the Sith* followed in 2005. The prequels got mixed reviews. Still, fans were happy to see more of the story.

STAR GAMES

Star Wars has inspired dozens of video games. The first LEGO Star Wars game released in 2005.

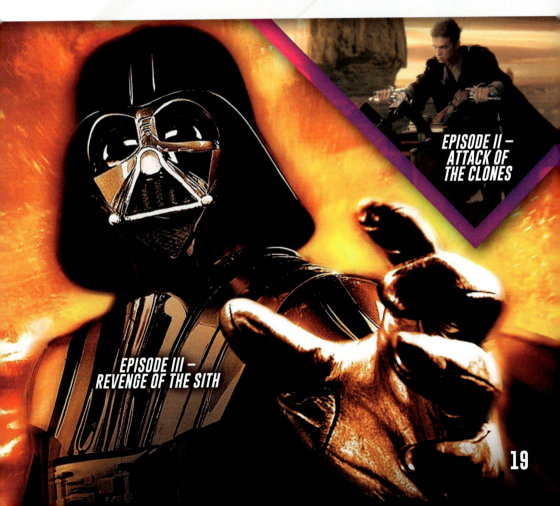

EPISODE II – ATTACK OF THE CLONES

EPISODE III – REVENGE OF THE SITH

In 2012, The Walt Disney Company bought Lucasfilm. Disney also announced the first new Star Wars film in a decade. *Episode VII – The Force Awakens* hit theaters in 2015. Fans met new heroes, like Rey Skywalker, Finn, BB-8, and Poe Dameron. The movie made $100 million in its first 24 hours!

REY SKYWALKER IN *EPISODE VII – THE FORCE AWAKENS*

FINN

BB-8

POE DAMERON IN *EPISODE IX – THE RISE OF SKYWALKER*

TODAY'S FAVORITES

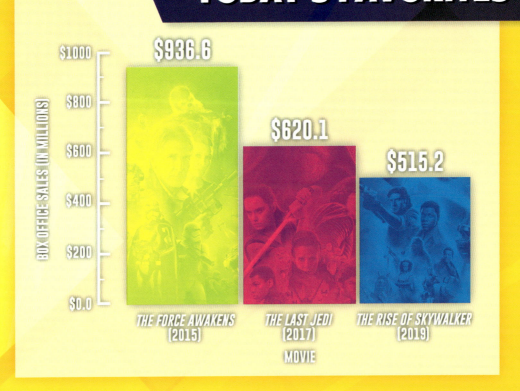

A STAR WARS STORY

Standalone movies tell the stories of Star Wars characters beyond the main trilogies. *Rogue One* was released in 2016. It earned more than $1 billion worldwide!

Episode VIII – The Last Jedi followed in 2017. Two years later, *Episode IX – The Rise of Skywalker* finished the trilogy. Overall, the movies had mixed reviews. But many fans were excited that they featured a more **diverse** cast than the previous trilogies.

STAR WARS TIMELINE

1977
Star Wars is released

1983
Episode VI – Return of the Jedi is released

1980
Episode V – The Empire Strikes Back is released

1999
Episode I – The Phantom Menace begins the prequel trilogy

2005
The first LEGO Star Wars video game is released

2012
The Walt Disney Company buys the Star Wars franchise

2015
Episode VII – The Force Awakens begins the sequel trilogy

2019
Star Wars: Galaxy's Edge opens at Disneyland and Walt Disney World

2022
Andor begins on Disney+

STAR TOONS

Animated Star Wars shows are popular on Disney+. *Star Wars: Visions* and *Star Wars: The Bad Batch* are fan favorites!

In 2019, Disney launched Disney+. The streaming platform began with eight episodes of a new Star Wars TV series, *The Mandalorian*. Viewers were hooked! They looked forward to new episodes featuring Grogu, a powerful child who looks like Yoda. A spin-off released in 2021. *The Book of Boba Fett* follows a popular Star Wars character named Boba Fett.

In 2022, the series *Obi-Wan Kenobi* became the platform's most-watched global premiere. Other Disney+ series, such as *Andor* and *Ahsoka*, follow other popular characters. Star Wars is full of entertaining stories!

GROGU IN THE MANDALORIAN

OBI-WAN KENOBI

USING THE FORCE

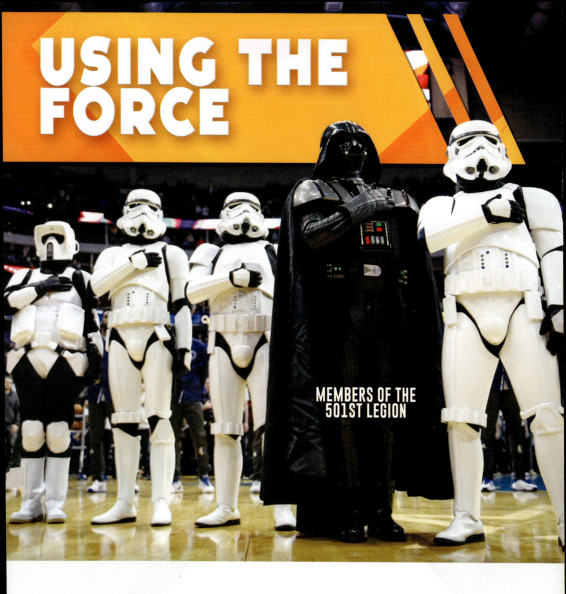

MEMBERS OF THE 501ST LEGION

The Star Wars brand uses its success to give back! Lucasfilm's Star Wars: Force for Change raises money for those in need. Since it began in 2014, it has given millions of dollars to organizations such as UNICEF and Starlight Children's **Foundation**. In 2019, Force for Change partnered with the FIRST organization. Together, they encourage kids to become leaders in science.

The brand encourages fans to give back, too. Groups like the 501st Legion and the Rebel Legion create realistic costumes and props. They attend events in full costume to raise money. Star Wars fans come together to make the galaxy a better place!

GIVING BACK

$1 MILLION GIVEN
TO STARLIGHT CHILDREN'S FOUNDATION IN 2017

OVER $9 MILLION
RAISED FOR UNICEF TO HELP FEED CHILDREN AROUND THE WORLD

OVER $16 MILLION
RAISED BY STAR WARS: FORCE FOR CHANGE SINCE 2014

CELEBRATING STAR WARS

STAR WARS: GALAXY'S EDGE
DISNEYLAND

There are many ways for Star Wars fans to enjoy the brand. Disney's Star Wars: Galaxy's Edge theme park opened in 2019. Visitors can explore a village on the planet Batuu. They can build droids, eat Star Wars foods, and meet popular characters. They can even ride the *Millennium Falcon*!

In 2022, Walt Disney World opened a new Star Wars attraction. Star Wars: Galactic Starcruiser is an imaginative adventure. Guests spend two nights living on a starship. They do lightsaber drills, pilot training, and more!

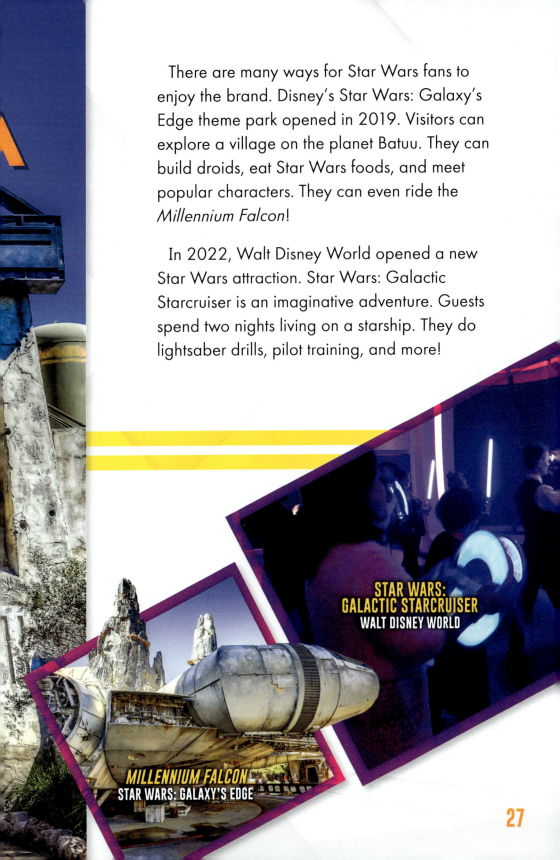

STAR WARS: GALACTIC STARCRUISER
WALT DISNEY WORLD

MILLENNIUM FALCON
STAR WARS: GALAXY'S EDGE

RANCHO OBI-WAN

STAR WARS COSPLAYERS

Collecting is also popular among fans. Many collect toys and other items. The world's largest Star Wars collection is at Rancho Obi-Wan in Petaluma, California. This museum has over 500,000 Star Wars items!

Conventions are the ultimate fan gatherings. Star Wars Celebration began in 1999. Now it is a yearly four-day event! Disney announces new Star Wars projects and stirs up excitement for future releases. Fans come together to enjoy screenings, news, celebrity guests, and **cosplay**. The Star Wars universe brings fans together!

BOBA BIG BUCKS

Rancho Obi-Wan features two Boba Fett action figures that fire tiny rockets. This is one of the rarest Star Wars toys. In 2019, one sold online for $185,850!

STAR WARS CELEBRATION

WHAT IT IS
A four-day event for Star Wars fans

WHEN IT STARTED 1999

WHEN IT IS HELD
At least once each year

WHERE IT IS HELD Around the world

ACTIVITIES
Fans can meet, learn Star Wars news, meet filmmakers, and dress up in costumes

GLOSSARY

alliance—a relationship in which people agree to work together

brands—categories of products all made by specific companies

CGI—artwork created by computers; CGI stands for computer-generated imagery.

conventions—meetings for people who share a common interest

cosplay—the practice of dressing up as a character from a movie, book, or video game

director—a person who controls the making of a movie

diverse—made up of people or things that are different from one another

empire—a group of people led by one ruler

foundation—an organization that gives money to people or groups in need

franchise—a collection of books, movies, or other media that are related to one another

galaxy—an area of gas, dust, and stars in space

headquarters—a company's main office

prequel—a story set before an existing work

rights—a legal claim to something

sequels—movies that continue the story started in a movie that came before them

space opera—an adventure set in outer space

special effects—effects that use makeup, special props, camera systems, computer graphics, and other methods to make fake things look real

trilogy—a series of three related stories

TO LEARN MORE

AT THE LIBRARY

Beecroft, Simon. *Star Wars Extraordinary Droids*. London, U.K.: DK Children, 2020.

Blauvelt, Christian. *Star Wars Use the Force!: Discover What It Takes to Be a Jedi*. London, U.K.: DK Children, 2020.

London, Martha. *Star Wars*. Minneapolis, Minn.: Kaleidoscope, 2019.

ON THE WEB

FACTSURFER

Factsurfer.com gives you a safe, fun way to find more information.

1. Go to www.factsurfer.com.
2. Enter "Star Wars" into the search box and click 🔍.
3. Select your book cover to see a list of related content.

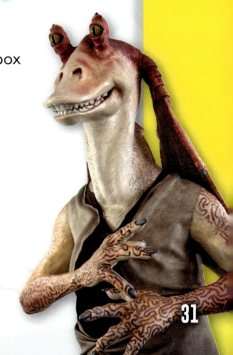

INDEX

501st Legion, 24, 25
awards, 13
characters, 7, 8, 9, 12, 13, 14, 15, 16, 18, 20, 21, 23, 27, 29
Disney+, 22, 23
early Star Wars earnings, 16
fans, 4, 5, 13, 14, 16, 17, 18, 19, 20, 21, 22, 25, 27, 28
giving back, 25
Industrial Light & Magic, 11
Kurtz, Gary, 8, 9, 10
Lucas, George, 6, 8, 9, 10, 11, 14, 18
Lucas, Marcia, 13
Lucasfilm, 6, 7, 8, 20, 24
movies, 5, 6, 8, 9, 10, 11, 12, 13, 14, 15, 16, 17, 18, 19, 20, 21
name, 9, 15
products, 5, 6, 10, 16, 17, 28, 29
Rancho Obi-Wan, 28, 29

Rebel Legion, 25
sales, 6, 13, 14, 15, 16, 17, 20, 21
San Francisco, California, 6, 7
special effects, 11, 18
Star Wars, 9, 10, 11, 12, 13, 14, 15
Star Wars Celebration, 28, 29
Star Wars Day, 4
Star Wars droids, 12
Star Wars: Force for Change, 24
Star Wars: Galactic Starcruiser, 27
Star Wars: Galaxy's Edge, 26, 27
timeline, 22
today's favorites, 21
TV series, 6, 17, 22, 23
Twentieth Century Fox, 10
video games, 6, 19
Walt Disney Company, 6, 20, 23, 27, 28

The images in this book are reproduced through the courtesy of: mark phillips/ Alamy, front cover (Stormtrooper); BFA/ Alamy, front cover (Grogu), pp. 12 (C-3PO, D-O), 15 (*A New Hope*), 21 (*The Last Jedi*, *The Rise of Skywalker*); Photo 12/ Alamy, front cover (Rey), pp. 12 (K-2SO), 13 (Chewbacca), 15 (Jabba the Hutt), 18 (Anakin Skywalker); Chris Dorney, front cover (Darth Vader); Art Directors & TRIP/ Alamy, front cover (movies); Patti McConville/ Alamy, front cover (merchandise); Oleksii Arseniuk, p. 2; Stefano Buttafoco, p. 3; Monkey Business Images, pp. 4-5; Jim West/ Alamy, p. 4 (Star Wars Day); Aflo Co. Ltd./ Alamy, p. 5; Lauren Elisabeth, p. 5 (lightsaber); simon evans/ Alamy, p. 6 (toys); Chris LaBasco/ Alamy, p. 6 (Lucasfilm headquarters); Miguel Lagoa, p. 7 (Darth Vader); f11photo, p. 7 (San Francisco, California); Featureflash Photo Agency, p. 8 (George Lucas); Lukasz Janyst, p. 8 (desert); TCD/ Prod.DB/ Alamy, pp. 9 (Flash Gordon), 21 (*The Force Awakens*), 23 (*The Mandalorian*); Cpuk/ Alamy, p. 9 (Gary Kurtz); Album/ Alamy, pp. 10 (inset), 11, 23 (*Obi-Wan Kenobi*); Moviestore Collection Ltd/ Alamy, p. 10 (behind the scenes); PhotoStock-Israel/ Alamy, p. 12 (R2-D2); newsex, p. 12 (BB-8); Everett Collection, Inc./ Alamy, p. 13 (*Star Wars*); Jon Kopaloff/ Stringer/ Getty Images, p. 13 (Marcia Lucas); Pictorial Press Ltd/ Alamy, p. 14 (*The Empire Strikes Back*); AJ Pics/ Alamy, pp. 14 (Yoda), 18 (Jar Jar Binks), 19 (*Attack of the Clones*, *Revenge of the Sith*); Ronald Grant Archive/ Alamy, p. 15 (Ewoks); Radharc Images/ Alamy, p. 17 (trading cards); Chris Willson/ Alamy, p. 17 (Kenner action figures); ArcadeImages/ Alamy (LEGO Star Wars); Dom Slike/ Alamy, p. 20 (*The Force Awakens*); PictureLux / The Hollywood Archive/ Alamy, pp. 20 (*The Rise of Skywalker*), 21 (*Rogue One*); Allstar Picture Library Limited./ Alamy, p. 22 (1977); James Wagner/ Alamy, p. 22 (2022); Tribune Content Agency LLC/ Alamy, p. 24; muzz_tafid, p .25; Jay Boncodin, pp. 26-27; Abaca Press / Alamy Stock Photo, p. 27 (*Millennium Falcon*); ZUMA Press Inc/ Alamy, p. 27 (Star Wars: Galactic Starcruiser); dpa picture alliance/ Alamy, p. 28 (Rancho Obi-Wan); Thusitha Jayasundara/ Alamy, p. 28 (cosplayers); Derek Teo/ Alamy, p. 29 (Boba Fett); Daniel Boczarski/ Contributor/ Getty Images, p. 29 (Star Wars Celebration); SERGIY ANDRUSHCHENKO, p. 31 (BB-8); Jeremy Pembrey/ Alamy, p. 31 (Jar Jar Binks).